Meet the Trumps!

An Introduction to America's First Family

Taffy Jensen

VANALDEN
MEDIA

You said to let the process play out.
And so it did.

Vanalden Media
18960 Ventura Blvd., #95
Tarzana, CA 91356

VANALDEN
M E D I A
www.vanaldenmedia.com

President Donald Trump was inaugurated on January 20, 2017, becoming the 45th president of the United States. That makes his family the "First Family" of the United States.

But who are they? Let's find out!

President Trump's wife is Melania. She is America's "first lady."

Melania Knauss was born in Slovenia, a country in eastern Europe. She came to the United States several decades ago as a fashion model.

Melania met Mr. Trump in 1998, and they married in 2005.

President and Mrs. Trump have an 11-year-old son named Barron. He lives in New York with Melania, where he attends school.

Barron is not President Trump's only child. He has two older brothers and two older sisters.

Nearly 40 years ago, President Trump was married to Ivana Marie Zelníčková.

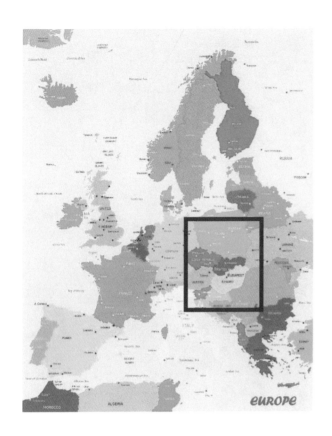

Like Melania, Ivana was from eastern Europe: she came from a country called Czechoslovakia. She and Mr. Trump married in 1977 and had three children.

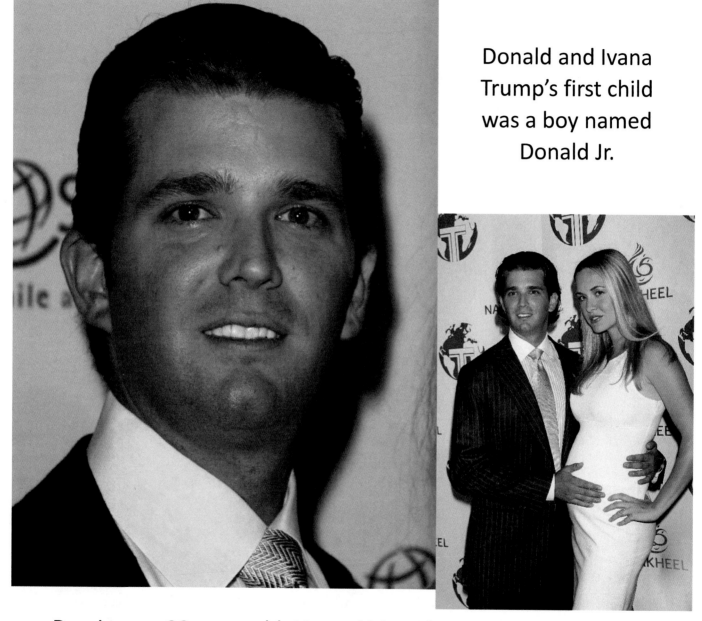

Donald and Ivana Trump's first child was a boy named Donald Jr.

Don is now 39 years old. He and his wife, Vanessa Kay Haydon, have five children (President Trump's grandchildren!).

Don Jr. works as an executive in his father's company, The Trump Organization. He helps oversee assets that are in a trust during Mr. Trump's presidency. Don Jr. also appeared with his father on his famous television show, "The Apprentice" on NBC.

The second child of Mr. Trump and Ivana is their daughter Ivanka, which means "little Ivana."

She was born in 1981.

Now 35, Ivanka is an accomplished businesswoman. She has served as an executive vice president in The Trump Organization and also has her own fashion lines and books.

Ivanka has also worked as a model and, like her older brother Don Jr., appeared with their father on "The Apprentice."

Ivana married Jared Kushner in 2009, and they have three kids (President Trump's grandkids!).

Jared, is a wealthy newspaper owner and real estate investor. He was a close and trusted member of Mr. Trump's campaign team and is now a senior advisor to President Trump in the White House.

Eric Trump is the third child of Mr. Trump and Ivana. Like his older siblings, he is an executive in his father's business and also appeared with the family on television. He founded the Eric Trump Foundation to raise money for a children's hospital.

Eric married Lara Lea Yunaska in 2014. They have no children.

The three oldest Trump children were active in their father's presidential campaign. They were strong, vocal advocates for Mr. Trump's candidacy. Ivanka in particular has been a close ally and advisor to her father and has now moved her family to Washington, DC, to support him in office.

Back in 1992, Mr. Trump divorced Ivana Trump. The next year, he married an actress named Marla Maples. During their six-year marriage, they had a daughter named Tiffany Trump.

Unlike her siblings who are based in New York, 23-year-old Tiffany Trump grew up largely in California. She is a recent graduate of the University of Pennsylvania.

So there you have it. With three wives, five children, and eight grandchildren, President Trump has a big family!

The Trumps stood together in support of Mr. Trump's candidacy for president, and they continue to show a united front as a modern American family... that just happens to be the First Family of the United States.

Now you have met the Trumps!

Photos

Don't miss Vanalden Media's bestselling introduction to President Trump. Because our youngest citizens are listening – and they have questions!

http://www.vanaldenmedia.com/djt

FOR KIDS, FROM VANALDEN MEDIA

Check out Taffy Jensen's other bestselling kids' learning books.

www.vanaldenmedia.com/TJ

FOR GROWN-UPS, FROM VANALDEN MEDIA

Hurrydate: A Speed-Dating Saga

Do you remember what it was like out there? This jarring, heartfelt bestseller details a woman's evening at a speed dating event and her quest for love, marriage, and children.

Mommy Haiku'd All Over the Baby

Know a mom? Gift her with this funny, dark, fast-paced, painfully relatable look at the reality of life with a baby. An Amazon #1 bestseller and Los Angeles Book Festival Honoree.

Mommy, Your Name is Poo Poo

Is there anything funnier than a toddler? Is there anyone more quotable than a preschooler? We don't think so either.

www.vanaldenmedia.com/CL

VANALDEN
M E D I A

ABOUT THE AUTHOR

Taffy Jensen is an avid reader and, in her spare time, a mother of three active children. She writes about the questions her children ask. And they ask a LOT of questions.

Made in the USA
Middletown, DE
22 July 2021